Friend of the Chimps

JANE GOODALL

by Eileen Lucas

The Millbrook Press
Brookfield, Connecticut
A Gateway Biography

Cover photograph courtesy of
Penelope Breese/Gamma-Liaison
Background cover photograph by Ginger Giles

Map by Joe Le Monnier

Photographs courtesy of Chris Boehm: pp. 4, 20, 26;
Carolina Biological Supply: p. 9; Photo Researchers:
pp. 12 (top), 15; UPI/Bettman: pp.12 (bottom),
33; C.S. Perkins/Magnum: pp. 19, 37, 40; Animals,
Animals: pp. 25 (top), 43; Anthro-Photo: pp. 25
(bottom, Richard Wrangham), 29 (James Moore);
Krasner and Trebitz/Gamma-Liaison: p. 44.

Library of Congress Cataloging-in-Publication Data

Lucas, Eileen.
Jane Goodall, friend of the chimps / by Eileen Lucas.

p.   cm. — (A Gateway biography)
Includes bibliographical references and index.
Summary: A biography of the zoologist focusing on her
work with chimpanzees at the Gombe Stream Reserve
in Tanzania.
ISBN 1-56294-135-6
ISBN 0-395-63570-5 (pbk.)
1. Goodall, Jane, 1934-   —Juvenile literature.
2. Chimpanzees—Tanzania—Gombe Stream National
Park—Juvenile literature. 3. Primatologists—
England—Biography—Juvenile literature. 4. Gombe
Stream National Park (Tanzania)—Juvenile literature. [1.
Goodall, Jane, 1934-   . 2. Zoologists. 3. Chimpanzees.
4. Gombe National Park (Tanzania)] I. Title. II. Series.
QL31.G58L83   1992
599.8'092—dc20
[B]   91-18060 CIP   AC

123456789 - WO - 96 95 94 93 92

For Linda Lowery Keep,
the bravest person I know.

Jane Goodall has devoted her life to learning about chimpanzees. Her studies of chimps in the wild made her famous.

Everyone at the London Zoo was excited. A baby chimp had been born that morning and was doing very well. It was the first chimp to be born in the London Zoo. Animal lovers all over England were happy to hear the news.

In a small town near London lived a woman named Vanne Goodall who liked animals a lot. To celebrate the birth of Jubilee the chimp, she gave her one-year-old daughter Jane a stuffed toy chimpanzee.

Some of Jane's aunts were afraid that the hairy toy would give the young child nightmares. But Jane loved her toy Jubilee. She dragged it around with her everywhere and held it close when she fell asleep at night.

Instead of nightmares, Jane had wonderful daydreams about chimpanzees and other wild animals. She dreamed of seeing such animals in the jungles and plains of Africa.

When Jane grew up, she made her dreams come true. As a young woman she went to Africa. After many years of hard work, she became famous for her studies of chimpanzees. She dedicated her life to learning about these animals and sharing what she learned with others. This is her story.

From the time she was a very small girl, everyone knew that Jane Goodall loved animals. The country village where she was born on April 3, 1934, was home to many animals. Jane was happiest when she could be outside with them. When she was two she was able to ride a horse at her uncle's stable. She never thought to be afraid of the large animal.

Jane also loved to watch animals. One day, when she was four years old, she crawled inside a neighbor's henhouse to watch the hen lay eggs. Jane sat patiently, without moving, until finally a round white egg appeared beneath the hen. The proud bird clucked with pleasure. And the equally proud girl raced home to tell her mother the exciting news.

Meanwhile, Vanne Goodall had been searching the neighborhood for her daughter. She was just about to call the police when Jane came dashing in. She was so happy that Jane was safe that she hugged the little girl and then listened carefully as

Jane told her all about the hen. Jane was very lucky to have a mother who shared her strong interest in animals!

By the time Jane was six years old, England was involved in World War II. Jane's father joined the British army. With bombs falling on London, Vanne Goodall decided to move with her two daughters, Jane and Judy. They went to live with Vanne Goodall's mother and sisters in a beautiful home called The Birches in the English seacoast town of Bournemouth. Jane went to school there. She was a good student, but she couldn't wait for weekends and holidays so that she could go back to being outside. Then she would climb her favorite tree in the garden and listen to the birds sing or go down to the beach to watch the sea.

When Jane was seven years old, she read *The Story of Doctor Dolittle,* a book about a man who loves animals so much he talks to them and takes care of them. She began to think about the different kinds of animals that could be found in the faraway places of the world. From this point on, she began to read every book she could find about animals. She began to think that she might like to study animals when she grew up. Perhaps someday she might even go to Africa.

Jane started a nature club with her sister and two other friends. They would go on hikes, and Jane would keep notes on all that they saw. The summer Jane was ten, they opened a museum at The Birches with all the treasures from their hikes on display. They gave the money they collected to a farm for old horses.

Jane loved to ride horses and worked at a stable so that she could be near them as much as possible. Once she went on a fox hunt. She had a wonderful time riding on a swiftly running and jumping horse. But when they got to the part where the fox was caught and killed, Jane was very upset. She never went on a hunt again.

By the time Jane's school days were over, her parents were separated. There wasn't money for Jane to go on to college. Instead, she went to secretarial school in London, thinking that with this training she could get a job anywhere in the world. She still wanted very much to go to Africa. But she hadn't figured out how she was going to manage it yet.

As a child, Jane loved animals. She dreamed of visiting Africa to see exotic wildlife such as zebras and giraffes.

After secretarial school, Jane worked at several jobs. Then one day a letter arrived from a school friend whose parents had a farm in Kenya. "Come to Africa," said the letter. Jane needed no further urging. What she did need was money, so she had to wait until she had saved enough for the trip.

Finally, in 1957, when Jane was twenty-three years old, she boarded a ship to sail for Kenya. Tucked inside her suitcase to keep her company was the little toy chimp named Jubilee.

It took three weeks to travel by ship down the west coast of Africa, around the Cape of Good Hope, and up the eastern coast to Kenya. Then there was a two-day train ride inland to the capital city of Nairobi. Finally, on the car ride to her friend's farm and on later rides through the countryside, Jane was able to see some of the wild animals of Africa close up.

And it was just as wonderful as Jane had dreamed it would be. She saw giraffes and zebras, elephants and antelopes grazing in the wild open lands. They were all so beautiful and so free. But it was not enough for Jane just to be in the land of wild animals. She wanted very much to study the animals and to understand them.

So Jane went to Nairobi, to the National Museum of Natural History, to see a man named Louis Leakey. Friends had told Jane that he might be able to help her. Dr. Leakey was a famous scientist who specialized in the study of the first people on Earth.

In Dr. Leakey's cluttered office, full of animal bones, thick books, and a large mouse cage, Jane explained her lifelong dream. Louis Leakey could tell that Jane was eager to learn, and he gave her a job as a secretary.

Some months later, Dr. Leakey and his wife went on a journey to Olduvai Gorge in Tanzania. They asked Jane to go with them. Olduvai Gorge is a place in East Africa where very, very old fossils had been found. (Fossils are traces of ancient life, preserved in rock.) Dr. Leakey believed that these fossils were the remains of some of the earliest people on Earth. He spent many years carefully digging in the area, trying to uncover the answer to the question, "Where did human life start?"

Louis Leakey at the Olduvai Gorge. Jane was thrilled to work with this famous scientist.

Dr. Leakey and his wife, Mary, examine pieces of a skull that belonged to an early ancestor of humans.

Sometimes, as Jane and the others worked, a rhinoceros would go plodding along a nearby dried-up riverbed. Several times a lion suddenly appeared in the bushes not very far from where Jane was working. Jane was terrified of the lion. But she knew how to back away slowly and quietly, without upsetting the great beast.

One night, after the day's work was done, Dr. Leakey told Jane about some chimpanzees living in the jungle of Tanzania. He thought that it would be good for someone to study these animals, which had little contact with humans. He believed that a study of chimpanzee behavior might answer some of the questions about the development of human beings.

Then he asked Jane if she might consider taking on the job. Jane was surprised because she did not have a college degree or many years of training for the work. But Dr. Leakey said that he was looking for someone who really cared about animals and the search for knowledge, someone who had an open mind and lots of patience—someone just like her.

Jane was very honored that Dr. Leakey would

consider her for this important and difficult work. And in her heart she knew that this was what she had been preparing for ever since she was a little girl. She gladly accepted the challenge.

There was much to be done to prepare for this project. Jane returned to England to talk to her mother about it. She also wanted to read as much as she could about the animals and the country in which she would be living. Dr. Leakey set to work to raise funds and get the necessary permissions. When some people in the United States agreed to sponsor the study for six months, Jane thought that everything was all set.

But then a snag arose. Local officials in Kigoma, the part of Tanzania where Jane would be working, did not like the idea of a young Englishwoman all alone in the jungle. They wanted her to have a chaperone—a companion who would watch over her.

Now what was Jane to do? Whom could she ask to come on this difficult, dangerous mission? Then Jane's mother offered to go with her. Jane was thrilled.

So it was all set. Vanne would keep an eye on

A chimpanzee mother and child. Before Jane began her work, few people had studied these animals in the wild.

things in camp while Jane was in the jungle observing chimps, and she would help Jane out in the evenings with her notes. And of course, keeping them both company would be a slightly tattered toy chimp named Jubilee.

The *Gombe Stream Chimpanzee Reserve* near Kigoma, Tanzania, was Jane's destination when she returned to Africa in June 1960. The Reserve was like a national park where the chimpanzees were protected. No one lived there except a few game scouts and some fishermen.

At Kigoma, Jane and Vanne boarded a small boat, which took them and their supplies twelve miles up the coast of Lake Tanganyika to the Gombe Reserve. The boat landed near a small fishing village on the shore of the lake, and the supplies were quickly unloaded.

A game ranger, two scouts, and Dominic, a cook Jane and Vanne had hired in Kigoma, helped them set up the two tents that would make up their camp. When the camp was set up, it was late afternoon. But Jane wanted to see a little of this land

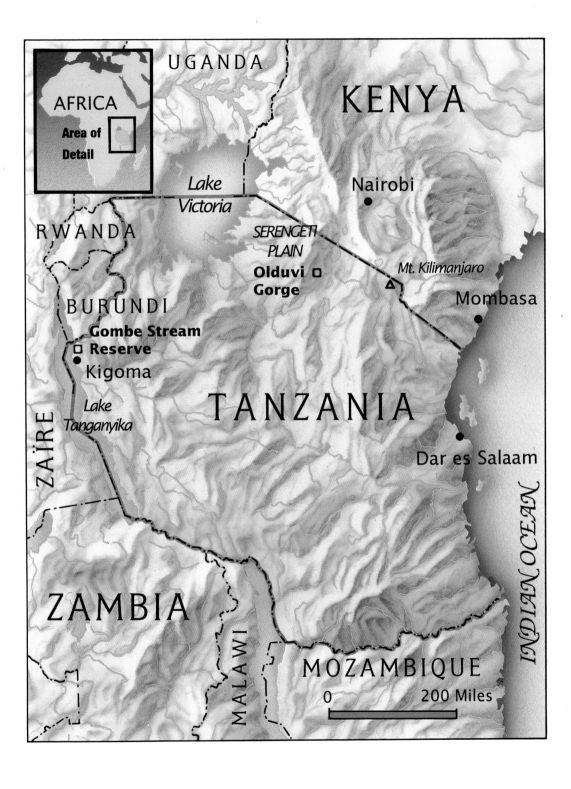

that would be her home for the next six months. From the shore of the lake, the mountains of Tanzania rose some twenty-five hundred feet. The slopes were mostly covered with thick forests. There had recently been a brush fire, and that made it a little easier to climb up the jungle slopes. But Jane had not gone far before she was filthy from slipping in the ash and dirt.

She did not see any chimpanzees on this first climb. But she did see some baboons, which hooted in alarm and ran off when they saw her, and a deerlike animal she knew was called a bushbuck. She was pleased to discover a good spot from which she could see for miles in several directions. She called this place "the Peak," and it would become her favorite lookout point.

Before dark she returned to camp, feeling good about her new home and the job she had taken on. That night she pulled her camp bed out of the tent and slept under the stars.

Jane was excited during her first week in the Reserve when she spotted chimpanzees eating the fruit of a tropical tree. Actually, she could barely see the chimps—they were hundreds of yards away

Jane at "the Peak." This spot became one of her favorite lookout points.

Chimpanzees in a fig tree. At first, the chimps at Gombe avoided Jane and refused to come out of the trees.

from where she sat peering through binoculars. Most of the time the thick branches and leaves of the rain forest hid them from view. But it was a start.

Jane hoped to get a closer view. But no matter how quietly or slowly she moved forward, the chimps ran away. So Jane kept her distance. She made careful notes of all she saw during the next week as that tree bore fruit. When the fruit was gone, the chimps moved somewhere else in the forest, and Jane could not find them.

For nearly two months she saw hardly any chimps at all. She could hear them, all right, screaming and hooting in the trees. She wondered if they were warning each other about the strange white woman-creature in their territory.

In an effort to find the chimps, Jane spent longer and longer days in the jungle. Every day she got up before dawn and stayed in the forest until dark. Sometimes she even slept in the forest, wrapped in a blanket on the ground. But still the chimps remained hidden. They were definitely avoiding her.

Jane began to get quite depressed. She was covered with insect bites and cuts and scrapes from climbing the mountains and crawling through the jungle. At night she took a bath in a canvas tub that was filled with spiders by the time she was done. In the morning huge centipedes crawled on the ceiling of the tent over her head. She had only six months' worth of funding, and now nearly half of it was gone with little to show for it.

Then, to make matters even worse, both Vanne and Jane became very ill with malaria, a disease spread by the bite of certain tropical mosquitoes. Officials in Kigoma had told them that there was no danger of malaria in this area. Thus they did not have the right medicine to fight the illness. For two weeks the two women lay in their tent sweating with fever. Dominic the cook did his best to take care of them and maintain the camp.

On the first day that Jane felt well enough to get out of bed, she dragged herself up to the Peak. Time was running out. She had to prove that her project was worthwhile.

Almost in reward for her patience, the chimps came out into the open that day. They still kept at a distance from her, staring as she perched on her rock. But they didn't run away. They quietly ate figs for several hours before disappearing back into the forest.

At the end of the day Jane rushed back to tell Vanne the news. Perhaps the chimps were at last accepting her presence in the forest. Maybe now she would be able to learn more about them.

In fact, over the next few weeks, Jane was able to learn a great deal more about the chimpanzees and their behavior. She began to understand the loose structure of chimpanzee society. In each group of chimps, there would be a leading, or dominant, male. Jane could spot him by his charging displays and by the way the other chimps groomed him.

Charging is a way in which chimps show everyone who is boss. The leading male usually has the most dramatic charging display. He runs directly at another chimp, stopping or turning away at the last second. Usually, he screams and makes as much noise as possible. A charging chimp is a scary sight indeed.

Grooming is a way in which chimps show respect or affection. One chimp gently parts another's hair and removes leaves, dirt, insects, and whatever else is there. Sometimes chimps will sit and groom each other for hours. Grooming is just one of the ways that chimps like to touch and be touched. They also hug and kiss.

Jane watched mother chimps play with their babies and young chimps play with one another. She saw how the chimps made nests in the trees to sleep in at night. Chimps make a comfortable sleeping platform by bending leafy branches one on top of another. When they wake, they leave the nest. They make a new nest wherever they happen to be when it is time to sleep again.

Jane also learned the many sounds that chimps make. One sound was a "pant-hoot" or "pant-grunt." The chimps used this and other sounds to greet each other, to warn of danger, or to let the others know that they had found food. When they were full and sleepy, they made a contented sound. And when they played, they made a laughing sound.

Over time, Jane began to recognize certain chimps that she saw often. She gave them names. She named the dominant male chimp Goliath, for

A grooming session. Grooming is a way for chimps to show respect and affection—as well as keep clean.

Chimps make many sounds to communicate with each other. Here, a chimpanzee delivers a "pant-hoot."

Jane takes notes as she watches a chimp family. She was the first to observe how chimpanzees raise their young in the wild.

his strength. Another large male she named David Greybeard.

And then there was Flo, a very motherly chimp. Her baby Fifi was always clinging to her as she walked through the jungle. Her son Figan usually followed close behind. From Flo, Jane learned how mother chimps care for their babies in the wild.

One day, as Jane's six-month study period was drawing near its end, she made a very important discovery. That morning, she spotted David Greybeard sitting in a tree. He was feeding on something, and several other chimps sat nearby. They seemed to be begging to share his food.

As she watched, Jane suddenly realized that David was eating meat—a young bushpig, in fact! Until then, scientists had believed that chimpanzees ate only fruits and plants. Jane was the first to see and record the fact that chimps sometimes eat meat. Later she would see that chimps sometimes hunt small animals for food.

About two weeks later, Jane made another exciting discovery. Again it was David Greybeard who let her in on a secret. This time she saw him poking a long blade of grass into a termite mound and eating the insects that clung to it when he pulled it out.

This was exciting to Jane because it was an example of an animal using a tool. After David left the termite mound, Jane went closer to examine the site. She plucked a fresh blade of grass and stuck it in the termite mound. Sure enough, several ugly, wiggly termites were clinging to it when she pulled it out.

Jane had made a practice of tasting everything that she saw the chimps eat, so she picked a termite from the blade of grass and ate it. She decided that this was one food she would leave to the chimps.

About a week later Jane saw some of the chimps making a tool to catch termites by pulling leaves off a stick. Many animals use tools, but it was commonly thought that only people could actually create tools. Later Jane would see the chimps create a number of kinds of tools. Besides "fishing" tools for catching termites, they made sponges to soak up water, by chewing on leaves. This meant that chimpanzees are even more like humans than had been thought.

A chimp uses a blade of grass to catch termites.
The baby will learn by watching.

These two observations—that chimps eat meat and both make and use tools—were very important. Jane wrote to Louis Leakey about them right away. Scientists in many places were excited to hear about the work Jane Goodall was doing. As a result, the National Geographic Society agreed to pay for Jane to continue her research for another year.

Jane was very happy that she could stay on at Gombe. She was becoming very fond of the chimpanzees. And there was so much more that she wanted to know about them.

While Jane was making exciting discoveries in the forest, Vanne Goodall had been keeping busy back in camp. Local people soon found out about her first aid kit and the gentle, kind way she had with people. They began coming to her with all sorts of medical problems. One of the local boys, son of a village chief, decided to be Vanne's assistant. In return for the many small tasks he performed for her, he was rewarded with bandages for his many minor (and sometimes imaginary) cuts and scrapes.

Vanne's presence was a great comfort and help to Jane. But after five months in the Reserve it was time for Vanne to return to England. Jane was sorry to see her go and missed her very much when she left. But it was not long before she was so busy with her work that she stopped feeling lonely.

During the next couple of months, Jane was able to get closer and closer to the chimps in the forest. Once a group of adult males surrounded her, hooting and screaming and even charging toward her. Jane was very frightened, for she knew that these chimps were strong enough to tear her to pieces. She forced herself to keep very still and pretended to be eating leaves. After a while the chimps went off and left her alone. She slowly walked back to camp, her knees shaking with relief and her heart beating fast with excitement at the thought of how close the chimps had come to her.

Another time a male chimp appeared in a tree above Jane and hit her on the head with a stick. Again, Jane remained as still as she could. The chimp soon disappeared into the rain forest. It seemed that the chimps had gotten over their fear of her and were now testing her. After several months of this angry behavior, the chimps slowly began to accept Jane's presence in the forest.

One evening, when Jane returned to camp, Dominic the cook reported that a chimp had come very close to feed in a nearby palm tree. The next day Jane stayed in camp. Sure enough, late that afternoon, David Greybeard appeared. Jane left bananas lying out, and David helped himself to some. Soon he was visiting camp fairly often in search of bananas.

David Greybeard's calm acceptance of the humans seemed to help some of the other chimps get over their fear. Soon some of the bravest would take bananas right from Jane's hand. No one had ever had such close contact with chimpanzees in the wild before. Jane had to be careful not to forget that these were wild animals.

In the fall Jane's sister Judy came to the Gombe Reserve to take some pictures. She was able to get some of the first photographs of chimpanzees using grass tools to catch termites. And when Judy returned to England, Jane went with her. Dr. Leakey had suggested that she study ethology—animal behavior—at Cambridge University. So Jane agreed

Fifi looks for bananas, which Jane sometimes hid under her shirt.

to leave her work to learn some things that might make her a better scientist.

For the next five or six years, Jane spent a few months each winter in England, studying and sometimes giving lectures. Jane was rather shy around people, and she found it hard at first to talk in front of a large group. But once she started talking about her chimps, she would get so excited that she would stop being nervous.

Each spring, she would hurry back to spend the rest of the year in Africa. Jane was happiest when she was studying the chimps. She enjoyed her time in England, but she couldn't wait to get back "home" to the Chimpanzee Reserve.

During this time, the National Geographic Society sent Hugo Van Lawick to photograph Jane and the chimps. Like Jane, Hugo Van Lawick loved and understood animals. Jane was happy to have the company of someone who shared her interests. When he left at the end of his assignment, she found that she missed him a great deal.

Then, shortly before Jane had to leave for her winter term at Cambridge, David Greybeard gave her a very special Christmas gift. On Christmas

Day, David wandered into camp, looking for bananas. As he ate his treat, Jane sat beside him. After a while, she slowly reached out and touched him. He actually let her groom his fur for a few minutes before gently pushing her hand away.

An adult male chimp who had lived all his life in the wild had actually let her touch him! It was the best Christmas gift Jane could remember.

The year after Hugo Van Lawick's first visit to Gombe, he returned to get more photos of the work being done in the Reserve. Jane and Hugo were very happy to be together again, and as time went on they fell in love. In 1964 they were married.

Jane had now spent some four years in the Reserve. She was able to follow the growth and changes in family groups in her chimpanzee community. Altogether there were about fifty chimps in her part of the Reserve, although they usually hung around in small groups of four to eight.

The adult female Flo, who had two sons (Faben and Figan) and a baby girl (Fifi) when Jane started her study, now had a new baby son. Jane named him Flint. Female chimps usually have babies about four or five years apart. That is about how long it takes for a baby chimp to become independent enough for the mother to take care of a new baby.

It was fascinating for Jane to watch the experienced Flo care for and protect her new baby. She could see how the youngster Fifi adapted to her new little brother and how the baby itself grew and learned. Then, when a younger female became a mother for the first time, Jane saw how this little chimp responded to motherhood. This was the first time anyone had made such detailed studies of chimpanzee society in the wild.

In 1965 the first permanent buildings were put up, and the Gombe Stream Research Center began to grow. Soon there was much more work to be done than Jane could handle alone. Assistants and students came to help with the work of studying and recording chimpanzee behavior. Now research could continue even when Jane had to be away.

Then, in 1967, Jane had a new demand on her

Jane videotapes a chimp outside the research station at Gombe, as a baboon looks on from the roof.

time. She and Hugo became parents of a baby boy, whom they named Hugo Eric Louis Van Lawick. Jane nicknamed her son Grub, a Swahili word meaning "bush baby." Like his mother and father, Grub loved the rain forest and the chimps.

Jane and Hugo made sure that their baby was safe by building a sort of wire "cage" for him to play in at camp. Chimps had been known to capture and kill baby baboons, and there were stories of chimps having killed human babies. Jane and Hugo were very careful never to leave Grub unguarded.

By watching mother chimps and their babies, Jane had learned a lot that was helpful to her in caring for her own child. She held and cuddled Grub as much as possible, just as a mother chimp does. And when Grub was trying to do something he was not supposed to do, she used the chimps' trick of distracting the child with something safe.

When Grub was nearly one, Hugo went on safari in another part of Africa to take pictures for the National Geographic Society. Jane and Grub went with him. As the youngster learned to walk and run and speak, he also learned about zebras and leopards. One of his first sentences was "Lion try to eat me," spoken after he heard a roar outside the family's tent. But he meant it as a joke. He was so unafraid of the wild animals that Jane and Hugo had to watch him closely. He seemed to think that the lions and hyenas were all his pets.

When Grub reached school age, Jane decided to hire a tutor for him at the camp rather than send him away to school. He would work on his lessons in the morning while Jane worked in her office. Then they would spend the afternoons together, "learning" about life in the Chimpanzee Reserve. Jane remembered how she had longed to spend more time outside as a child. She wanted her son to have the chance to do just that. She knew that there would be plenty of time for Grub to go to "regular" schools when he was a little older.

In 1968 a tragedy occured at the Gombe Stream Research Center. A young research student named Ruth Davis did not return to camp one evening. A search party was sent out immediately, and after six days of searching the young woman's body was

Jane watches chimps at Gombe. Her observations have shown that chimpanzees behave like people in many ways.

found at the foot of a cliff. She had fallen and been killed instantly. Ruth's parents agreed that she should be buried at Gombe, in the mountains of Tanzania that she loved so much. It was a very sad day when she was laid to rest in the Reserve. Her death reminded the growing number of people there of the dangers involved in working in the wild.

The study of the chimps went on. Jane and Hugo were often apart. She needed to be in the Chimpanzee Reserve, and he needed to be all sorts of other places taking pictures. With their careers keeping them apart so much of the time, the marriage became very unhappy. In 1974 they were divorced.

Jane then met an Englishman named Derek Bryceson. He had spent many years in Tanzania working to protect the rain forest and its wildlife. Once again Jane was happy to have the companionship of someone who cared about animals and nature, and soon they were married. When Derek died in 1980, Jane was deeply saddened. But her life was very full, with much to learn and much to teach.

Today *Jane Goodall* still travels to speak in many places. She has written books and articles about her work. And she has worked hard to spread knowledge and understanding of wild animals. As part of this effort, she founded the Jane Goodall Institute for Wildlife Research Education, and Conservation in 1975.

Work has continued at the Gombe Stream Research Center. Sometimes people ask Jane if she doesn't already know everything there is to know about chimps. She answers that it took years of study just to know what questions to ask. And she is still discovering things.

Over the years, Jane has become concerned about the future of animals in the wild. Every year there are more people in the world—and every year people take over more wild areas. Then the habitats, or homes, of wild animals are lost.

Jane has also become concerned about the way people treat animals in captivity. She is especially upset by poor treatment of chimps and other animals in zoos and medical research laboratories. Sometimes mother chimps are captured and killed

Captured chimps like this one are often treated badly.
Jane has pressed for better treatment of captive animals.

On speaking tours, Jane tells about her work at Gombe and urges people to care for wild animals and the places where they live.

so that their babies can be sold to zoos and research labs. And sometimes the captive animals are kept in tiny cages and treated cruelly.

Jane has spoken out against this mistreatment. She also started a project called ChimpanZoo to promote better treatment of chimps in zoos. As zoos around the world become involved in the program, they may help people everywhere learn more about these animals.

Jane Goodall has devoted her life to understanding animals. Today she is working to help people understand that they must care for animals and all the natural world. Human beings are already the most powerful creatures on Earth. Now we must learn to be the most responsible.

Further Reading

Chimpanzees, by Prue Napier (McGraw-Hill Book Co., New York, 1976).

Tracking Wild Chimpanzees, by Joyce Powzyk (Lothrop, Lee & Shepard Books, New York, 1988).

Goblin, a Wild Chimpanzee, by Geza Teleki and Karen Steffy (E.P. Dutton, New York, 1977).

The Chimpanzee Family Book, by Jane Goodall (Picture Book Studio, Saxonville, Mass., 1989).

Grub, the Bush Baby, by Jane Goodall (Houghton Mifflin Co., Boston, 1970).

My Life with the Chimpanzees, by Jane Goodall (Pocket Books, New York, 1988).

Index